Animal People

*I.M. Yurij Georgievich Drobyshev, b. Leningrad,
June, 1932, d. Pentir, Gwynedd, November, 2015.*

Animal People

Carol Rumens

Seren is the book imprint of
Poetry Wales Press Ltd.
57 Nolton Street, Bridgend, Wales, CF31 3AE
www.serenbooks.com
facebook.com/SerenBooks
twitter@SerenBooks

ISBN: 978-1-78172-318-0
ebook: 978-1-78172-319-7
Kindle: 978-1-78172-320-3

A CIP record for this title is available from the British Library.

The publisher acknowledges the financial assistance of the Welsh Books Council.

Cover Image: Joseph Albert "Wettlauf des Igels und des Hasen, 1862"

Printed in Bembo by Latimer Trend & Company Ltd, Plymouth.

Author Website: www.carolrumens.co.uk

Contents

On Standby

Pass me that small pencil, sharpened nicely
At both ends, a pencil with two eyes,
And up for anything – a screed, a scribble.
The gold and navy stripes, still visible,
Might be school uniform – the low-slung tie
Of anti-fashion, mocking and awry.
The pupils do their time; some pencils sidle
Off desks and drop and vanish. But the word
Is out, this pencil says, when a bright-voiced
Young teacher names the mist in someone's head.
And the kid stares, and sees the point at last.

A pencil starts from scratch, like anyone.
It knows hard graft, despair and knuckled tension,
A shadow flickering like a footballer's –
Designed for transfer. It diminishes,
But leaves hard copy, proofed by crossings-out,
Forensics of the rubber, and the bruise
Of graphite on our fingers. If you've never
Nibbled at a pencil-top, you've never
Tasted words.
                    Pass me the pencil! Yes,
I'll leave it by the keyboard, just in case…

An Artistic Family

We were girl-wives with an idea of beauty so simple
it featured cushions and coffee-mugs, and, once,

the matching of wallpaper to high aspiration –
a frieze. On bands of coarse cord-trim she pearled

French knots – pale green on blue, maroon on grey; she plotted
hearth-rugs in black-and-white geometries famous

as Modern Art. I favoured stripped-pine floorboards,
clashed with acrylics; she preferred Axminster's

Turkey-red with the dark-oak Jacobean
of nineteen-thirties marriage. Both of us relished

the irony of Woolworth's 'wrought-iron' planters.
She liked to quote what a teacher said about her:

"She'll have a beautiful home. She's so *artistic*."
The beauty we could buy was decoration's

trivia, and we laughed about that, too.
"If you want a beautiful home, marry a wealthy man."

Neither of us did, but we went on being artistic.
I see it, more and more often,

and farther back: – the drip of Liquid Lino
on the beaks and wings of her customised Flying Ducks,

the squirrel buttons, blue, for a girl's first cardie,
and the delicate green-and-gold Greek-key design

of our famous frieze, the best in the Wallpaper Book,
lifting the child-long day in her tiny dining-room.

Easter Snow

*"There was a man of double deed
Sowed his garden full of seed…"*
                      Anon.
"And so I've found my native country…"
                   Attila József

There was a man of double deed
Sowed his garden full of snow,
Lit a stove he could not feed,
Sired a child he could not grow,
Who fashioned birds from wooden blocks,
And when their wings fused flight to dark,
And when the dark swept through the locks,
Fetched a book and made an ark.
But who could sail so deep a ship,
Or marry beast to bolting beast,
Dance as he would his flimsy whip
Over the backs of the deceased?

Poets must tell the truth, you said:
The poor must, too, although they lie.
We listen at your iron bed,
Under the tunnel of the sky,
And ask you softly what you need –
Blue roller-skates? A football team?
But you are far and far indeed.
And all the stumbling magi bring
Is the smoke-haze of a dream,
A floating girl, a greasy bear,
A courtyard echo-echoing
The snowy wing-beats of your heart
Towards the deficit of air
Predicted in your natal chart.

The Teacher and the Ghosts

after *A Christmas Carol* by Charles Dickens

There were two, a boy and a girl.
He tried to say they were fine children
but the words choked. *A lie of such magnitude.*

This boy is Ignorance. This girl is Want.
He sat up, startled. The room was itself, bright;
the time on his wrist as it should be.

Boxing-Day trade outside. Girls and boys
in their smart affordable brands,
shopping, texting, playing; time

on their side. *Beware them both and all*
of their degree but most of all beware
this boy. He shook off the lie. They were fine children.

Spring Forward, Fall Back: a Gwynedd Skein

milk-tooth   eirlys
an earth-cub's yawn

soaked his black fur
beneath iâ du

frost on our ffos
                by noon
                      frogspawn

       *

field-alchemy   manichaean
   miaren   girlfights
harts-tongues and horse-tails
  in the green ash-grove
grasshopper   doorbells

       *

     slow grass horse
   gwinau march
fall-back pegasus
   bear our particulate
     wherever birches ride
       branchy in the blue

       *

first on the moon
on the bare draen du
a single redstart

the day I leave
let clouds cancel
    the looking-back   these
                  mountains

Spring Forward, Fall Back – mnemonic for BST clock-adjustments.
Cymraeg: *eirlys* – snowdrop, *iâ du* – black ice, *ffos* – ditch, *miaren* – brambles, *grinau march* – chestnut horse
draen du – blackthorn

11

The Homeless Ship
(seen from the Bangor–Chester train)

Coastline of caravans, neat as graves, but quieter,
rank on rank of them, with a permanent way
like a peace-line slicing through: inscrutable classifications.

The borderlines of property: recession.
Washed-out-tired of looking across a too-
small sea, we blank the peninsular horizon.

A factory fizzles dry, the land reverts to grazing,
and there's our ship, beached, ruminant, rusting.
It fell in love with the wrong colour of pastoral

and now it waits for a tide that never comes near,
bleak as the child in the inland caravan
or an emigrant, detained. His palms and shins

are skinned to roaring salt, he can only shake, and go on
surfing the lorries, night after night, believing
that this is the night he'll cross the sea to England.

March Morning, Pearson Park

for Maurice Ruherford

Victoria, so young, so white, so modern
for 1854, seems reassured:
the people in the People's Park deserve her,
and, revels quarantined by calico
and carriage-drive, have earned their prophylactic –
beef, beer and Madame Genevieve's rope-trick.
"The foot is free-er, and the spirits more
buoyant when treading the turf than the harsh gravel"
said Zachariah Pearson, speculator,
bankrupt shipper and philanthropist,
who squared things with his conscience, on reflection,
bath-chaired beside the unattractive lake.

In early spring the trees' wrung hands implore
winter to stop it; the forsythia's tiny
oilskins drip, and the bedding-plants are sat
in rows in railed-off, graveyard rectangles,
dim-eyed as board-school children. If they blossom –
a primula here, a dwarf iris there –
the only colour's royal, unreal purple.
Two teenagers beside the listed fountain
play some new kind of netless badminton.
The bright white fan-tail of their shuttle-cock
takes off, lands, takes off, its flight-path slow
as slo-mo through the February-ish air.

Remote Bermudas

1. School Trip

We're bunched at tables we're too long for.
You beckon me over.
I praise your map,
and wonder if the green-fringed shape
is a spice island in the Humber
that'd taste like rum baba.

We part the squamous sea. We're outward bound,
happy as coloured pencils to have found –
pace the rage of the prelates –
this archipelago of tender states.

2. Keats's Reach

His name flowed here eventually; it was seen
in the sand-green shallows,
in the scrimshaw, bitterly tiny, left by bodies
who'd nowt to say to the night, the bridge, each other.
It bubbled up like a greasy
bin-bag playing at lungs.
It was only a name. Happen it died easy,
one steadfast star, the usual Venus, trembling.

3. The Campus of Time-Enough

The world and time were green, and up to us –
literature students, geeky mutants, born
beyond the age of literature and students.
The broad-leaved foliation of the fittest
draped the roof-beams, and, from what remained
of roof, flowed weedy gardens,
impossible to mow. The lecture halls were host
to mites and stalagmites. Ideas were moss
in board-rooms without windows, let alone Windows.
Still in our early teens, it seemed we were
wrinkled as tortoises, so shy and slow,
we'd never kissed. We'd never said hello.

4. Lumen de Lumine
(after Edgar Bundy's 'The Night School')

His pillar of Biblical gold
is leaking height,
its tallow hollowing out
like faith in a too-industrious
lily-of-the-field.

He's making notes on oxygen and light,
and that stor thing
where Workers of the World Unite,

fired-up, though hope's all nesh and scant.
Is there a thorny crown
in this religion? Or a bended knee?

Sometimes, it's like he's been laid off again,
to yell and scuffle on the quay,
wild with an agony of entitlement.

Yorkshire words:
Nowt – nothing
Stor – great
Nesh – cold

The Big Bang Year

We were the world again
in the Big Bang Year, in the roar of Twenty-Thirteen,

with all our Queens of Sport, and our sport of a Queen.
Long may they reign!

Out there, the gas-giants barely caught a whiff.
Black holes stayed resolutely negative.

Hot Jupiters squashed pesky particles
and learned to make small household articles;

Old Saturn clocked a flash but did he spot
the precious few, the precious wotsit in a silver…? Not.

Our infra-red was trending nowhere dark
for all the calories in that Stratford park.

But God, who hadn't started anything,
seemed newly plausible. We heard Him sing:

"Behold! Marbled Londinium, striding plain
through fire and plague and politics. What fast-lane

shipping! what towers and Thames! what artful riding
of horses on the hillsides, what a tiding

of tourists and their web-cams. Didn't I create you,
Brand Britannia? If not, I hate you!"

He vanished then, with British lack of fuss,
like doping rumours and the extra bus.

A legacy of little meteorites
twinkled down the sky, for the few nights

the weather held. *Magnificent hopes unstopping*,
we told ourselves. Then it was winter: rain,

power-cuts, filthy footprints. Almost sane,
we crossed out "empire" and continued shopping.

Her to Apollo

I fall in love and sunbathe less these days –
I must be old, the bark-legged woman says.
Stuff your Olympics. I'll be in my black,
pissing on you, Apollo. But the star
that spikes earth's drinks and rapes her slow, sings back,
my face is all you got, bitch, all you are.
The woman spreads her thighs. Such green light beckons,
and gods, however cracked, must claim their tokens

from flesh that knows it's trees and cloud and slate,
and not too tall to stretch a prayer. Gold pieces
wink in her eyes like birch-leaves, ripple out
like baby cephalopods. And still he lies,
that god – *I'm all you need, I'm all you are;*
your genesis, baby, and your nemesis.
He oils her richly, and turns up the power;
she's barbecued, and calls it paradise.

Iron insouciance that dawns with love's
self-love, and gilds earth's have-nots into haves,
you win, she thinks, and sees next autumn scatter
the little, light-stunned faces, plain as scars,
and as unique – each leaf uniquely spoiled
by cell-death, yet each death the same. Who'll matter?
Apollo, know yourself – you're gas, not gold,
and one of around two-hundred billion stars.

Glosa on 'Woman of Spring' by Joan Margarit

Behind words you are all I have.
It's sad never to have lost
a home because of love.
It's sad to die surrounded by respect and reputation.
I believe in what happens in a poem's starry night.
Joan Margarit, tr. Anna Crowe, from
Tugs in The Fog (Bloodaxe,2006)

Once, you looked love at me; I saw no hatred.
I must have been the world's worst reader of eyes.
Sorry your nice-girl smiles were mistranslated:
you never would have fobbed me off with lies.
It was the myth I was tending, Heroides,
Harrods, or simply "Let us live…"
Melody of the thousand cadences
behind words, you are all I have.

When the gods partied, cataracts of fable
poured from your stained pitcher, my statuesque
Iris, a little bruised. Creeps fawned at your table,
warm as the ill-kept wine, and assessed the risk
of an infidelity, shifting shadow by shadow,
and when they heard a fluttering in the grove
of your heavy furniture, they said It's sad
never to have lost a home because of love.

Yellow beacons are feathering the hill,
planted by those incorrigible suitors.
Your children are dutiful,
quarrying stone, they say, for your new headquarters,
and one day you will ride
out on the shining shoulders of your nation.
If I'm still in the crowd, I'll grin. It's sad
to die surrounded by respect and reputation.

We'll never again meet, and, if we could,
I'd make the same adrenaline mistakes –
panic, nausea, mortification, red
startled to white, the high chant of Sapphics:
Oh, let the apple nod
towards the sunburned hand, bringer of blight.
I myself was once ravished by a god.
I believe in what happens in a poem's starry night.

Two Birthday Cards

1. Under Moel Rhiwen

Sam, 6

Your sky, my sky
seem the same –
smoke-drifts, pearls,
feathers of snow.

The years stream
their weather. Yours
are bare new hills.

Climb. Climb slow

2. White Night

Yura, 80

Peach without a stone –
dense silver flesh
faintly ashen.

This night's almost
other-night taste;
dawn-dry sleep-thirst.

Warm. No shadow.
Voices and dew-fall
of Letnyi Sad.

Your half-clear face
in the small darkness –
summer's lease.

Fire, Stone, Snowdonia

Like the fireworks at the beginning
   of time and, perhaps, its end,
holiday cars rip past our field, each slow

controlled explosion leaving
   the giant white ARAF signs
bemused, extinguished,

as if a world were englished
   by acceleration.
Each tiny ton retracts,

on the bend, to a glob of snail-shell,
   a lovely silence, fraught
with the patterns of language.

In the acre he'll never till
   Boreas, unabashed,
works out. He could bucket the lot –

four-by-fours, the rolling rugs of cypress,
   cottages limp in their nets
of Scottish Power. But for now

he's happy enough to harass
   a riot of buttercups, kettled
in rye-grass left to the sky

by a passing strimmer's witty
   attempt at scenery.
Gold in a glister of snow –

what more, as a lover of lowered
    sights, could you wish for?
The field has fallen castles

of dry-stone wall, dim mines,
    velodromes, auditoria,
slate-veined, fluvial, plosive

with fern-drips. Listen. Tune
    out the traffic. Ear-ball the Ipods,
of insects, the beetle-techno,

the muted maracas, the crackle
    of wings while the fossil-fuel shines.
The shyest grass aims upwards,

but the ways of the insects
    are horizontal.
Like us, they are slow kissers.

Like us, they phone-hack, thieve
    bonuses, see colours
others can't, and meet themselves

in sudden horribly familiar
    eye-studded hammerheads, tarmac-black and fiery
as petrol, old and wicked as the wind.

Praying with the Imam at Summerfade

Willow herb   jasmine   convolvulus   wild roses
We know what America brings us,
the Imam sings, *America brings us roses*
And Europe flings us jasmine.
We know what flowers they bring us.

I'm ashamed I can bring so little –
only this old Welsh text, illuminated
white and red, earth's litany, autumn-muted.
The shiny, weak, bright-stemmed convolvulus
spirals round the stalks of the rose-bay willow.

And they forge the usual wild embrace, the swaying
deadlock of equals, yet
both are in flower; the day's sufficiency feeds them.
Bees are scarfed in gold   the goldfinch misted silver

willow herb   roses   jasmine   convolvulus   pray for us
ac yn aur ein hangeu.

Cymraeg: *ac yn aur ein hangeu* – now and at the hour of our death
(from the *Ave Maria*).

The Reddish Wheel-Barrow

So much of it's rust,
it would disappear between traceries of rust,
were the rips and holes not laced
with additional strips of rust.

It might have lost its lustre
building the future –
the *tachka* pushed through rainwater and rocks
in the *lager* – grim artlessness –

but now it's an installation –
almost the Doctor's prescription:
so much depends on a sieve
that doesn't let everything through,

*

Beside the barbarous
wood-pile your red
sweat-shirt,
your axe-blade, small and bright,

champing at the boughs –
birch and ash, your elbows
patched up with tartan:
raz   dva   tri   chetire,

seli, vstali, seli, vstali –
that old-style Soviet drill
craved and hated by
the sweat-lit body.

★

Steady dissection. Birch and ash in knotty
bone-heaps: radius, ulna, fibula, tibia,
a few curled fingers
of leaves. The wheel revolves,

soundless of axle, sound of tyre,
the wide bin before you,
weightlessly gliding, wearing
its firewood thatch

and you, my love, my learning-curve
in the notion of keeping light
and close to the detail –
not to dilate upon love

or *corrective labour*, but find
one midsummer night in a moonless
Gwynedd ditch, the slight
possibility of an oven.

What more do you need but a Zippo
to lick the ziggurat over,
the flame-saplings wriggling
at gusts from the rusty air-ways,

red heat, white ash and always
someone to share the business
of chicken-breasts, blush tomatoes
and peppers, glazed?

★

So much depends
upon
juxtaposition –
the gears of a poem-in-motion –

or simply *hyperteria monokyklou*,
wintering upside-down against the wall
for as long as gravity wants
to play, and white feathers fly

from important sacrifices:
for as long as we fetch and carry
tyre-shreds, cinders, rust
at the edge of a rusting spade.

Notes:
Tachka – (Russian) wheebarrow
Lager – labour-camp
Raz, dva, tri, chetire – one to four count used in aerobic drills, etc.
Seli, vstali – sit, stand (as above)
Hyperteria monokyklou – (Greek) – "one body for a one-wheeler."

Happy Seventieth Birthday Blues, Mr Zimmerman

I'm staring into seventy, staring at that old bad news,
Yeah, staring into seventy, staring at the rank bad news.
I'm getting slowly smashed, but it's not the getting smashed you'd
choose.

It's a wall that's got no garden shining on the other side,
A wall that's got no pardon, smiling on the other side –
Just ask any angel who ever crossed that divide.

I heard the devil singing, he was singing to me long ago,
He sang me through the sixties, he sang me years and years ago –
Sang *Man, if you're a woman you just have to grow and grow.*

I'm a long-born woman, and it's the shortest straw.
I'm a long-born woman, smoking my cheroot of straw.
But I'm no damned angel, I was born to be a whole lot more.

I'm looking at the wall. Are you telling me it's a gate?
I'm looking at a wall, yeah, he's telling me it's the gate.
You can find it if you're blind, baby blue, it's not too late.

We're only ever twenty, we're only ever at the start.
We're only ever peddling that iconic parabolic start.
And there's no wall, baby, it's the shadow of an empty heart.

Go cruising into seventy: seventy's a broad highway;
Cruise along at seventy, along that broad highway –
You'll soon be doing eighty, if the angels get out the way.

All Souls' Saturday Night

In the corner of my living-room, she'll sit
watching herself on TV
lost in a vision of mobility
which doesn't hurt, or almost doesn't hurt –

they said I was cut out to be a dancer.

Foxtrot, waltz, tango, samba, rumba –
the glitter-balls revolve:
a ghost of taffeta holds her, slips her on –

doctors should kill us off when we get to sixty.

She swims the air
with swollen broken-slippered feet; her see-through
hands drift to unlock
the rack of hips: she stands, she's twisting free
in the shudder of a beginner's paso doblé,

and steps out partnerless   who needs a man
to kick-in the glass, glissade into a streaming
of stars across space-time to be
her own blue heaven? There's the empty chair –

you should have seen me at the Hippodrome

and in my living-room, her quick-step quickens,
lightest among them, and the glance
over her shoulder knows I'm watching her
somewhere, on television.

Owls of the Ukraine

Oookh-ooookh

Vooookh-vooookh

The unpatrolled
new pairs roll out

conversationally
their smeary cry.

It feathers away

above the moonlit

helmets, the man-rage:

*Khokholi, Khokholi
Moskali, Moskali*

Note: the first two word-pairs are Russian owl-hoots, transliterated in English: the last two are, respectively, Russian insults to Ukrainians and Ukrainian insults to Russians.

The Search

I.M. Annie Mills, neé Clarke, and her brother, Horace

Remembrance Sunday on a small TV
in Grandma's room: her vase of red and gold
'chrysanths', her tissue-box. The piebald cat
sprawls on the floor with one ear pricked, like me,
half-troubled. "They shall not grow old, as we…"
But how can Grandma's brother not grow old –
the round-eyed soldier in the round tin hat?
He was sixteen, he swallowed a big lie,
and told one of his own, and took the pay.

He's barely present at 'The First World War
Remembered' exhibition, but the crooning
from scratched shellac, of *Keep the Home Fires Burning*,
reminds me of my father – how, each year,
when the long guns marked the eleventh hour,
indoors or out it was our cue to freeze.
"Stand up! Stand still!" Why am I saying these
same words to him? His cheating home-fire's ash
while I'm still trying to catch his voice. I wish

I'd kept his voice.
                        I drift towards a keyboard:
Horace Clark, I remember. With an *e*?
I add an e, click *search*, and the command
wakes up the screen, and floats on its North-Sea-
blue, a raft of text. "Battleship – the Nelson.
Able Seaman – aged nineteen – died
1917. Cause unknown."
It's plainer than a student's record-card
but it's the door he steps through to this world.

I closed the page, already trembling – Christ! –
he'd said my name! He spoke broad Kentish, too.
He wasn't pleased to be so vague a ghost.
"Cause unknown? I'll give 'em cause unknown."
On Sunken Road, I felt his face, the crust
of beard, the Clarke snub-nose. *He said my name.*
Great Uncle Horace, woven out of you,
my mind makes this…

                    Of course, I'd search again,
thinking I'd bring him closer, ten years on.

I've trailed him through a roll-call which displaces
certainty with a hapless regiment
of Horace Clarkes, ascending as I scroll,
hauling their kit of birthdays, home addresses
and deaths (if known), all marching with intent
not to return. They fall, they re-enlist,
and swirl like snow beyond their own retrieval,
the screen too small, the distances too wide,
now the last living memories have died.

John Rodker Composes a Cold Elegy
for Isaac Rosenberg

no more will that pronoun in your sealed hand
nor the tricks of your verb–wires   trip me

no more shall the brush-fire   you sowed   fanned
                           sweep by & gut my   dirt-town

     flirt on   whip of stars   red heap
            alas my lipless!
                see
your miraculum   your misillery   crackle   into closedown

Pyramid Text

When the king wants the war,
The soldier wants the war.
When the soldier wants the war as the king wants it,
The war loves the soldier.
When the soldier wants the war as the king wants it,
War loves the kingly soldier and the king's god loves him.
The army shines from the south, its swelling river
Spreads glittering sky all over the hard fields.
The soldier shines from the south, he wants the kingdom
As the swelling river wants it, spreads his glittering torrent
Over the rocks and drenches the hard fields
With sky, and scatters stars of grain: when the soldier
Wants to become the seed, the soldier sows the kingdom
In corn so tall it reaches the king's shoulders
And bends its ears as he whispers
Bring me the bread of war. Bring me the soldier.

Zootoca Vivipara

The lizard taketh hold with her hands
and she is in kings' palaces,

the spectacle of her accomplished
evolution a tiny
fragment of bronze-blue mosaic
after an explosion,

her species older than the birds,
and closer to the stars
that are still very close, and molten
behind their rays,

a juvenile *vivipara,*
her fore-hands lifted
in a last, eloquent gesture,

who touched the Permian desert
and the Anthropocene,
where she sticks, flat as a stamp,
in her new little suit of lights.

House Clearance

Won't it be fun to turn into our possessions!
Let's practise. I'll be the cheese-grater:
you be a cutting from *Argumenti i Facti.*
No, wait. I'll be the roll of mildewed carpet
budging up for the toppled chair
which is you, with four stick-arms raised in goodbye.
What about that striped beach-towel
whose stripes have gone with the beach?
You can be him, and get wet.
I'll bare my ribs and be the heated rail.
What thick steam we'll make!
If you'd rather rust quietly, hook
yourself to the ceiling,
and I'll be the cowbell I bought
from a woman who was turning into her earrings
in a shop called 'Evolution.'
Listen. Let's just be jars,
glass, empty, unlabelled,
fully recyclable.
The kids'll take our tops off, shake us, sniff.
What disappointed faces!
Either no-one guesses
it's us, and we're sort of joking
or they just don't find it – sorry –
funny. Seems we're obliged
(once more) to humour the children.
No jars, then. Let's be footloose

instead, and try on these
time-crazed, gravity-addicted,
browner than bullshit slippers.
With eyes in our heels, and a soft
hissing that could almost
be waves, we'll synchronise
my quick, your slow, to a nice
andante. Who could bear to dump
such good, leathery people?
We'll glide, waggle, circle
like house-sharks, sometimes even
pretend to bask, our fringed mouths slightly open –
four of us now, sipping at the future.

Song of The Obsolete

Once there was much to be made, much to be made, much to be made,
Much to be sold to be sold to be sold;
Much to mix, mash, mould, much to split, splice, spoil, much to catch, much to carry,
    And you in the mills and mines and millinery rooms
Was small as a coal and twisted
And cheap as a lie but the labour
Was bread and you kept at it kept at it kept
At your keep, your bare keep, the bare earnings you'd barely keep.

Now what's to make, mister? Sister, what'll you sell?
You hated us didn't you hated us didn't you hated
The handles you heaved, the treadles you waded, the windlass that wound you.
    But now where's the hoist for your hope?
Where's the job, the five bob, the slick rob, the quick sob, and the picketline's glory?
    Don't look at us don't look at us don't look at us.
We'd give you the works if we worked. We don't work. End of story.

Where are the bastards that built us, the slavers that skilled us —
The pay-packet packer, the docker with dockets, the stacker of profits, the stockist?
What are our hours, now it's time that maims and mills us?

Home Thoughts from the Cow-Shed

for Yura

When streets and signs reclaimed Cymraeg, our pad
spat out its Saxon – Pinfold – and became
Buarth Gwarchau (native speakers say "Bith Gwar-kai.")
Both names had lustre, but the hard-to-tame
Welsh was the one to brag about with friends –
English friends. *It's cow shed, cattle yard.*
So it suits us! And so it strangely did.

Sinking, weathering, stiffening, wind-erupting
like *gwartheg* ghosts, we settled for the subtle
exchange of birch-tree and boletus, grass
and flesh. The farm dissolved into its sideline
of caravans, but when we lived here first,
March brought, along with daffodils, the fine,
black, yellow-tagged bull-yearlings, and their lust.
They'd snort and shove and tear the gorse; at night-time,
stand quietly in the ditch, and look at us.

The farmer up the road has plans to graze
two horses in their empty field. He patches
the fence with crates. The hawkweed will be sowing
new stars, and harebell sky will frame our riches
a little longer. Both of us were blow-ins
but you, by dying here, became a native –
(although you never learned to say "Bith Gwar-kai").
I'll find some new *boleti* where the birches
and fungus share their sugars of decay,
remembering with what care you'd delve your pen-knife,
so that the spores might fruit another day.

Cymraeg – the Welsh language
Gwartheg – cattle

Figurine

(Calcite, Ain Sakhri cave, c.8000 B.C.)

Heart of a calf, composed
of two mini-humans,
their bumpy heads the atria, scant limbs
like wraparound arteries,
it sat in your palm. Deep in a storm of bloodstreams,
the mouths and noses puzzled: kiss or breathe?

★

Were you fondling a floating rain-queen, or
the golden one inside you, your
double undoubled, coupled as if never,
till someone, you, remembering, knew this cobble,

★

pushed into the sparkly calcite grain
made memory stand again?

★

Not all the harsh-gasped breathing-to-breathing, not
all the clench and sweat   not all
the corn-silk adhesive   not
the bleeding and delving   not all
        the arching   the wrenching   the splitting   the
                sweet, oh, the sweet rain sowing
        the replica heart, whose thin cry you were crying
could have sheltered you from our mouths.

★

Rain speckled museum pillars. Slow red buses.
Laughter, raincoats, silliness, stillness.
But thy eternal summer shall not

★

Their whistle-thin bones, their sand-grains of saliva
deep in the flotsam of Ain Sahkri: here.

★

So long lives this. I wish you could hold your lovers
(I wish *I* could) – blunt-headed, froggy-legged,
sighing and moving together,
with centuries to discover how to breathe.

Danae, Dinarii

'As wolves love lambs, so lovers love their loves'
(Phaedrus, Socrates)

The pursuit of Immortality, bragged the Poet,
was nothing! I was young
and showered with starry faces.

Not divinities, he said – these were people:
boys, girls, much alike – just people –
the same lizard brains, the same jack-hearts,

the same unbeatable-value profiles, lips
shopping around for kisses.

They've crumpled now, he said. They smiled too much, got scaly
or soft. But the originals,
pocketed at the moment

the mouth my own had touched
sang from the fire, are hard and fine and sovereign.
Savings, he grinned. *Poets' currency.*

It's Time for the Weather!

Blizzle lightens to *waterbud* before strengthening to *pluvoria*
& *seaflay*   later *smogmer*   steadily thickening to   *notabretha*
    summerlonglast is *fade* becoming *saturbang*
    bangfrice brings plummeting temperatures
the outlook's *katabase*, followed by rising *hellglow* *humitude*   and a
dowly prospect
            of *glumtideyule*
        buy your solar credits now if you're worried about
            allyeargridoffswindlemas
        Enjoy the rest of your evening!!!

A Christmas Stocking

Mitts, with a reindeer pattern
across the knuckles,
a colouring-book, a fan
of Lakeland pencils,
a hollow bird, which, filled
with water, burbled
as long as you could blow –
what didn't that 'stocking' yield
when frisked from welt to toe?

It wasn't long before
I guessed who peered
at midnight round the door.
I knew no sleigh careered
down the pink London sky,
answering every cry
for bikes or kittens.
The times were tough. And cold.
I'd have to wear those mittens!

Whatever time might teach,
nothing could cancel
the hope renewed in each
strangely-shaped parcel
wedged yearly in a fawn
school-sock. I watched it dawn
with morning's grey, or groped
the black-out, pouncing on
the magic as it slept.

Now, at the frowsty heel
of years, I stretch and feel
farther for paper's scratch
on wool. And sometimes, still
that blend of things foreseen
and not yet spellable
unwraps my mind. I catch
some sharp, sweet Christmas smell –
and there's the tangerine!

Happy Christmas, Sister Dympna

"Animals *are* people!" Sister Dympna feeds the camera
that twinkly look she got through being chosen
from all the whining, wagging, weaving strays in the enclosure
to be Love's Guide-Dog and the Nation's Anchor.
She can't keep cats. Or terrapins. They're people
and she's reserved for God. A venial sin, you say,
this heresy, but what does Pope Francis say?
Has God agreed to a new species-steeple?

Animals don't have souls. Horns, hooves, et cetera,
aren't suited to the sacred menagerie.
No pets, no God, I thought. I had a hamster
I loved and taught some tricks and challenges,
claiming her (airborne in a basket) First
Hamster into Space. And when she died
(in bed and full of hamster-years) I cried.
I'd been a little beast; my skin was fur, reversed.

In those days, mice could sew, dogs dance, and fuschia piglets
with hats and ginghamed picnic tables perved
our childhood dream of childhood. Animaddictive,
Tom was an evil psycho, and deserved
to be cat-pancakes. Dragons, less than furry,
grinned *ranckes of yron teethe*, burned fossil fuel, and crunched
Anglicans, till we charmed them. Then, like us, they lunched
on salad, muttering "Hurry, oysters, hurry!"

Sister Dympna prays for the word-lords who engrave
small discs with "Dots-Toyevsky", "Mopsy-Mow"
or "Prince." In her new series, *Boss and Slave*
(the Christmas special, *Hoping it Might Be So*),
she steals the keys to all the Pets-at-Home
cages, and – is she dreaming? – whispers, "Run,"
before she kneels, on cue, and finds the new-born Son
curled in his hay, blind as a kitten, bless Him.

Small Facts

The cold snap holds –
  hardly a flicker of wing,
  or sprinkled seed of song.
Cars on the narrowed hill
  are slow and few.
All creatures hide or die
  from snow…

  It blazes at the door
  with a gaze to crack
thin glazing, bricks un-braced
  for zero – but not you.
This severer takes no part
  in your heart-lessened pace,
your sightless turn towards
  the mystery-journey's
imminence… What journey?

And when – (still warm – but when) –
  you're filled with cold,
out in your unprotected
  bed, where earth is heaped
in scarp and fold,
  I'll know not to mistake
the mottling grass or clear
glitter of song or wing,
  for some molecular soul –
what's soul? – re-entering
  earth's atmosphere.

Fact: I shall not re-make
  my snow-man beliefs,
  nor think it consolation
ever that you – or any
  creature in its un-making –
  "quietly"   "sleeps."

In Memory of a Rationalist

A man lies dressing-gowned among his arguments,
dying, pitiless. His head feels small
and analogue, unlike the instruments
which live his life, now, with sad lack of style

or appetite. On digits, thoughts depend –
a circuitry they find profoundly facile.
Sparing his friends the presence of a mind
un-catheterised, he schemes to shake that vessel.

He picks his question (answerless, in the end)
and waits. Not like old songs, but sharp as gods they come –
Explication, Comparison, Example,

Exhortation – Olympian athletes all,
sparring through morphine's bland encomium
as he yells quips and insults from the trainer's stand.

From an Evening Walk–Diary

New width of light, you warn me
how near mid-summer is, how soon these hills will drift
into old shade. No player-season, wild
in his carbon mask, has quite undone the year.
Spilled blackthorn, early stitchwort,
along the banks might have been snow doilies,
until last week, when I heard the sheepfold stream,
all February a loud-mouth,
began to sigh and doze.

There are new arrivals, young-voiced in the lanes:
some crouch with beer-cans by the road to Rhiwlas:
a girl runs, with a bud of bright light swinging
between her breasts.

Slow spring dusks, you remind me
of the last lap of age, how stretched and fine the days there.

Marshalsea Quadrille

1.

Debts stacked up like bricks,
at the Tabard as I lay,
watching a chink of sky
from the slushy sticks

the Surrey side of the Thames.
Debts stacked up like bricks,
and sundry heretics
and smugglers came to terms

but the pauper's room cost double
when the gaoler threw a six.
Debts stacked up like bricks,
the bricks stacked up like trouble

and toppled on the pricks
who'd have chucked them back (fair's fair)
if they'd not been starving where
debts stacked up like bricks.

2.

At the Tabard as I lay,
saving for my salvation,
the criminal population
tripled in a day.

I counted out my cash
at the Tabard as I lay
and then it rolled away.
I heard a distant splash,

but, loaded, didn't care
what load I couldn't pay
at the Tabard as I lay
and prayed some good soul there

would buy my round-e-lay,
and underneath the tap
would thrust his little cap
at the Tabard as I lay.

3.

Watching a chink of sky
he passes Nancy's Stairs,
not knowing they'll be hers –
only that good souls die

un-saved by gilded towers,
watching a chink of sky.
He gulps a ha'penny pie
with a few fanciful tears.

Some grubby gargoyles that
might be debating why
watching a chink of sky
concerns this sewer-rat

jeer as he scuttles by.
To Lant Street, then, and home –
contented in the gloom,
watching a chink of sky.

4.

From the slushy sticks,
a London Particular
snuffs Perpendicular
to smoking wicks.

He often walks all night.
from the slushy sticks,
to skin his cicatrix,
his blister-pack of light,

and save the child who drowned
although he'd learned some tricks
from the slushy sticks –
the child who won't be found

by any politics
or power that snivels pity,
but never walked to the city
from the slushy sticks.

A Few Study-Notes

"Stone walls do not a prison make,
Nor iron bars a cage;
Minds innocent and quiet take
That for an hermitage." (Richard Lovelace, 'To Althea, from Prison')

1.

I couldn't sleep. I'd got back late from the Ministry,
bruised by linen-board and letterpress –

old, heavy, well-made lamps I'd found in the darker stacks –
but had kept the wicks unlit, afraid of questions.

It was like a gourmet meal, prepared for no-one
(a tenant child, perhaps, an errant husband),

sure to congeal unhappily and revolt
microbially. I went outside. The moon

was lost, the clouds like half-cooked Yorkshire pudding.

*

The full blaze was a double chrysanthemum
I'd never seen before, mottled with blackfly.

Pulsating, blood-supplied, it was the mirror image
of an uncorrected lens. I leave it uncorrected

since everyone knows what the full moon looks like.

*

The wind was cool, then cold as scholarship.
The lamps stood unconfined in various bivouacs.

I drank some year-old grapes, and turned to you, my four-
centuries-old convicted Royalist.

Richard, your lines were danceable, but burned me –
that footnote like a detached retina.

I sleepily revolved the aesthetic question
but couldn't solve it: is it "gods" or "birds"

that wanton in your hand? I wonder what you hear
in Althea's hair-thin whispers through the trickle

of sewage, rain and rust. Outside, there's war,
England's blown chrysanthemum, riven with gods and birds.

2.

At the Ministry, I'd found a plastic out-tray
had replaced my wooden nest-box –

now with a different, younger name on it,
other white eggs inside it.

What are you trying to tell me, Minister?

What was my nest-box, anyway, but a cuckoo?

★

The Prefecture, some four li north of here,
has pizzerias and happy hours and nail-bars,

and stacks of broiler-boxes. New translators
work on the tongue of this year's press release.

The Prefect-Scribbler writes, *You will enjoy the mountains.*
Here, we feel free. His eloquence delights him.

★

When the migrant young fly in, the Ministry
pats its hard pockets. *I, too, like to eat.*

Hatred sizzles across my paths like bush-fire.
I stamp it down: opaline ash-curls, flight-feathers.

The Prefect grabs at the phoenix, almost strangles it.
He has no blaze, no neck and an eternal smile.

3.

Wind in the silence. Words. I sometimes meet them.
They never begin by asking for a light,

never return a text: they chew their lips
like stubborn children who confide their day

only if you desist from questioning them,
or else keep up a stare

so long you see the first pond-water eye
hair-pricked by sunbeams, pinned until it seeps

a retinal cell, and another retinal cell
and what it sees would have been called "amazing"

if any mouth had formed, or any mouthing.
When word-suns shine, it's not philosophy.

*

In the eggshell dawn, the courtier climbs alone,
takes No-Guide Path, and Hard Way

and Ankle-Twist Path and Downhill and Re-Track,
and sleeps in the common tanning salon, pillowed

on quartz. He has no Personal Development Plan.
By the king's humility, and the poet's translation

of stone and iron, his lamp is fed and lighted.
Flutter of doodled cupids, escaped birds...

Fly, dear Richard, footloose Cavalier.

His dance-steps fade in cloud-wisps, maiden-hair.

Hamlet
(freely after Boris Pasternak)

The noise died. I stepped onto the stage.
And now I lean against a door-frame, tense,
Keyed up for cues, the mutterings of events
Rehearsing the performance of the age.

The deepening dusk's thousand binoculars
Take aim at me, point-blank along the one
Axis. Not a blink. If it can be done,
Father, Abba, I beg – *let my cup pass.*

I love your bloody plots, I'd willingly
Take any part you offered, except this –
The part you're writing now. The scenes unfold

As planned, the actors strut their entrances.
And I'm alone, crushed by the Pharisee.
"To live a life is not to cross a field."

The Ship of State

After Brodsky, after Horace, translated from the Russian
with Yurij Drobyshev

Fly with the waves, little ship-of-state.
Your sail's a crumpled rouble-note.
The republics scream from the hold's throat.
And the planks complain.

The plating buckles, the sea swashes,
The helmsman blabs about man-eating fishes.
The bravest mouth is sick of dishes
Thrown up again.

Mad as a bullet, with less of a goal,
The storm's got lost in its rock-and-roll.
Don't worry, old ship – even the gale
Hasn't a notion

Whether to rush to this side or that –
Four sides have become the norm, in fact;
This could be a Hyperborean's flat
Overlooking the ocean.

Fly, little ship, and don't be fazed
By cut-throat rocks. Your hull might graze
An isle, where crosses bleach on the graves
Of sailors, where

Bundles of letters are to be sold
By a surprisingly blue-eyed child –
Flower of a native's century-old
Love affaire.

Don't trust that congress of officers
Generally known as guiding stars;
Attachment to the idle mass
Can hurt your head.

Trust the one thing of solid worth –
The waves' democracy, its froth
Of lively speech, its contact with
The ocean-bed.

Some sail away to forget disgrace,
Some, to insult Euclidean space;
A third group vanishes without trace.
They are all one.

For you, little ship which Borya steers,
There's no horizon other than tears.
Fly through the waves until you're theirs.
Fly on, fly on.

Footnote

Canto XXVII, Purgatorio, *The Divine Comedy*, Dante

How much it matters to be taught and fed –
early or late or anywhere in life,
to walk bent low and listening to the dead,
rather than stalk a Ghibbeline or Guelf
or the exemplum of one's dazzling self.
Dante knew: to be taught is to be fed.

He'd slept too long. Now dawn exposed the bluff.
He leaped the rock-fall, lighter than his years
and Virgil reached a hand to him, and said
"You must go on alone from here." Each stared
into a face that, quicker than the stars,
was gone. And Dante wept, still child enough.

Three Fado

freely, from the Portugese

1.

There was a sadness
lit up the city.
Not one person
returned my gaze.

Maybe I dreamed it –
a gate flown open,
iris to iris
one blue gaze.

2.

Among deceitful shadows
When far-off stars were breaking,
We gave each other roses
To forget we ever gave them.

To forget we ever gave them
We gave each other shadows
When far off stars were breaking
Among deceitful roses.

Gypsies, green young gypsies,
Give us that song again –
Sins are boys of twenty:
Regrets are deaf old men.

3.

You that wash clothes in the river,
You that chop planks with machetes,
Cutting my coffin to size –
There are rich boys who'd save you;
Buy up the land God gave you,
But your life, nobody buys.

At the round table, singing
We drank from the bowl that circled
With covert kisses and wine.
You gave me water and berries.
You shared your feast, but the bread
Of your life, nobody buys.

I sleep in the simplest bed,
Pressing my cheek to the mud,
Heather and bracken my blanket.
I lie where poverty lies,
And you bless the rich boy with sweet incense,
But forgiveness, nobody buys.

You that wash clothes in the river,
You that chop planks with machetes,
Cutting my coffin to size –
Some say money will save you;
But I have a life to give you,
The life nobody buys.

Laundry Blue

freely, after Attila József

The creaky, loaded basket at her hip,
Mum took the wash up to the drying-attic
and I, a poet even then, stayed back
to stamp around, and make my feelings known.

My howls meant, 'Mum, don't leave me on my own.
Don't hug those babies when you should be hugging
me!' Mum didn't take the slightest notice.
She went on lifting, stooping, reaching, pegging
sheet after glistening sheet, slip upon slip,
darned socks, gradated nurseries of the headless,
and dancing shirts. That's how poor women love –
with pegged lips and an ounce of indigo.

The wet shades still flit and flap above.
I try to rub my tears off, to compose
my roaring face, and…
But Mum can't hold me now. Her grey hair blows
across a sky of rain she's mixed with blue.

The Hare and the Hedgehog

after 'Der Hase und der Igel,' *Children's and Household Tales,*
Brothers Grimm, *1857*

Who will bury the hare,
the hare left bleeding by the hedgehog's cheating?

He and the hedgehog raced down the field. The hare
was ahead, had almost won when he heard
the shout, "I'm already here."
He ran back up like a whirlwind,
Heard "I'm already here." Ran down. "I'm already here."
Ran up. "I'm already here."
Need I go on? Need I go on?
But he went on, the hare.

Thirty times, forty, fifty…
He's tired, and the tiredness comes
from a new planet of tiredness,
but his head, full of blood-pump and wildness,
can't work anything out,
can't get at an obvious question
like, "Why is that hedgehog so fast
on his laughable trit-trot legs?"
Or, "Is there another hedgehog in this field?"
(as there was, a Mrs. Hedgehog).

Fifty times, sixty times, seventy, seventy-
one, seventy-two, seventy-three…

He was crazy, of course, this hare –
so fast on his one-track feet, so sharply sure,
even flaked out, blood leaping
from ears and eyes and the curled-back lips, brain spinning,
he laughed with his hare-self, winning.

The hedgehogs snorted and grabbed
the prize – one coin and some brandy –
like the swindling peasants they were.

And the heart-broken, beautiful hare
seethes in the nettles and sun, melts in the rain and the root-work,
until you can say, Oh, sure –
this is a story. There was never a hare.

On the Spectrum

You look back at your life, or up. It's a winter night
clear-skied. One constellation figures bright
and nameable, and makes the darkness right:

the constellation Art (or Maths or Science or
Loveable Eccentricity, if that's what you prefer).
It's the articulation of the best of what you were.

You pull the sharp-edged stars into a fat bouquet;
you know the gods are idiots, but, being human, pray.
You tell the children, 'These are roses'. What else can you say?

You look back at your life, or up. The moonless sky's
old book of knowledge is a research exercise
where experts thoroughly expose your expertise.

You're wrongly psyched, sad poet! See, the dark's unsigned –
no glittering sword and belt; your metaphors, slipped rind,
one twisted-metal star-collision mirroring your mind.

★

No more the one-letter pronoun   no more the tricks of your verb-trade
all is intransitive only   the child picks asphodel

Never your fingers quick on the obsolete harp   and the torches
flowing in amber streams   over the days   gone out.

What is retrieved or remembered? Have you a jar for the fountain?
Have you a small enough jar   for the ash of your being?

★

Much is misplaced as shadows cross the white light of the temple.
Dismantle the neurones, God. Then try to find your image.

★

A kids' party is foreign languages
screamed at you as she as you as he as you run about the little island
no boats are visiting for the next thousand years

★

Tired. Say that. She was tired
or say she tried

tried it and tired it for sixty years   tried it on
till a moment ago, a quarter to
                                        now
tried to edit it all to all right   all righted   again a
gain   We ride it   till twenty past trying   till
the final date with

★

Sleep, my little almond, my little nut-case

and rest   ever-unknowing
not even a moth-mouth chasing you
not your own thumb
                            testing you   inch-worm   petal.
Sleep, little Neanderthal

No species learns from dying how to do
death well   not even Brother Human

★

On the bomb-site there was a fox
stretched mid-leap   the leap made sleep   un-muscled
in the quick blue fly-light

I was afraid of words that bled   but I could look at death
kindly, and keep its fur-shred   knowing it little as love

★

How does those girls know the same secret and say it
how are their sharing without it words or why
is the hair so bright and pale and what are they laughing?

★

You know, of course, not to make the being-sick face
if They have sausages roping out of their nose, not to laugh if They
are eating tissue-paper from space-blue hands

not to screw your finger, snigger the scare-word *mad*
although *They* are, because they're a Mongol Child
(Are you catching their mustn't-say madness?)

You know when someone cries, like your arm's afraid of their shoulder,
like your skin shrunk   you go hollow-sick and grey –
crybaby sobs – you don't know who. Is it *You*, like? Or, like, *They*?

★

I listed all the pieces, with all their Köchel numbers,
and listened to them all, eventually.
I got to know the 212 emotions
as well as Mozart knew them –
the tiniest modulations, the accidentals,
which keys might tell a girl "love"   and make her wet
despite the ink on her lips, the notes all over her fingers.

★

She a mask, a gash, a lapse, a chromium hasp.
She paintstrips you with her pashes, her clasps soon grasp.
Her aspie-friends fiisk with her (gasp!) on the ticklish cusp.
Her jam's a stash, her sleep a wisp. Her dance beats brass.
She's Pandora's whirling cache: adze jigger axe saw screwdriver rasp.

★

AM: Aliens Onset.
In a seat, solemn,
ET's animal-nose
Emails a sonnet:
"Am I a stone lens?"

Male-ant noises.
I'm sanest alone
Online at a mass –

O silent as amen.
"I am a stone lens."

★

If we had friends, we'd think
fifty years without a word essential

If we had money
there 'd be days we'd blow the lot on party selves.

★

Over your little lives like the bodies of birds,
I called the winds of my love-and-art affairs
to scatter leaves, sweet leaves,
and apples and new handkerchiefs.

It was autumn though I didn't know it
because the wind smelled kind
and the dry leaves smelled of life,
and you weren't dead at all, but running, untouched,
towards your indestructible horizon.

I see you now for the last time, sentinel
in the iron branches over the iron bedstead
where I lie as I always lay,
solitary, naked, trying
to be covered by a wind of green kisses.

★

There could never have been a lover –
my love is not fitting.

Nor a child for my Poundland cradle –
my love is not fitting.

Nor a mother-and-father for my Judas kiss.
They had *True Love*. My love was never fitting.

But when I pray, is there nothing
unborn enough, unasking,

unseeing enough, enough
away to want no small-talk?

If it has heard of itself
it hears no news of our damage.

It is the *Unbeloved*:
the truth we have never failed,
who makest us also immeasurable.

Who art within our syndrome.

About Animal People

The final sequence of this collection, 'On the Spectrum,' explores from a female perspective some of the effects and affects of Autistic Spectrum Condition (ASC). My purpose was to present vignettes of a woman's life, partly my own, as poetic documentary. Current research has found evidence of gender differentiation in the way the condition presents, but many more studies will be needed in order fully to understand autism in females. In the meantime, women on the spectrum are often stereotyped according to the diagnostic criteria of male autism – which may also be stereotypical. Personal testimony – even a poet's – has a place in enlarging the view.

Autism may be associated with genes which have been passed down through the intermarriage of Homo Sapiens and Neanderthal Man, and originate from the genetic make-up of the latter. The variant gene DRD47K is thought to be implicated. There is some evidence that AS individuals, male and female, have an unusual affinity with animals, and, judging from the behaviour of my family and friends "on the spectrum," I find this credible. For people so often embarrassed by mis-communication, and stigmatised by the kwikfit attributions of literal-mindedness and want of empathy, the notion of an ability to form special cross-species relationships is certainly an attractive one.

We're all animal people in the broader sense, of course: as Bertholt Brecht wrote:

I'm friendly to people. I put on
A stiff hat like they do.
I say: they're animals with a quite particular smell.
And I say: it doesn't matter, I am too.

('Of Poor Old B.B.' Tr. Peter Lach-Newinsky)

'Autistic individuals with a narrow focus of interest and a high capacity for technical thinking and pattern recognition would easily filter into specialized roles in the technological and natural realms as their gifts would make them inventors of technology, keen observers of pattern in weather and in animal behavior, as well as star gazers and calendar makers. The rigid and analytical thinking of such people could lead to the breakthroughs in human behaviors which reduced resource stress and increased longevity, ultimately leading to population increase. Indeed, such thinking could be taught to others who themselves were not autistic yet were perfectly capable of following a standardized method of observation and behavior.' ('Autism, the

integration of "difference" and the origins of modern human behavior.' P. Spikins, Cambridge Archaeological Journal, 2009).

"Neanderthals were the original rebel rock-stars." Garret LoPorto, *Huffington Post* blog, 27.2.12.

Acknowledgements

Thank you to the editors of the following publications, in which some of these poems, or earlier versions, first appeared:

The Reader, The Rialto, New Walk, TLS, Poetry Review, PN Review, The Yellow Nib, The Manhattan Review.

The Captain's Tower: Poems for Bob Dylan at 70 (Seren) *Saudade: An Anthology of Fado Poetry* (Calouste Gulbenkian Foundation), *Inspired by Hungarian Poetry: British Poets in Conversation with Attila Jozsef* (Hungarian Cultural Insitute), *Festshcrift for Fleur Adcock.*

A Mutual Friend: Poems for Charles Dickens and *The Arts of Peace* (both from Two Rivers Press with the English Association, Ed. Peter Robinson),

'Easter Snow' appeared in *The Best British Poetry 2014* (Eds. Mark Ford and Roddie Lumsden, Salt, 2014.

'The Owls of the Ukraine' was posted by me on Billy Mills's Poster Poems, Guardian Books.

The poems set in Hull were written for a range of local writers' and university-based projects, organised by Cliff Forshaw.

'Song of The Obsolete' was nominated for a Pushcart Prize.

I am grateful to my patient and caring editor, Amy Wack, and to the following friends who commented briefly on various poems-in-progress: Desmond Graham, Philip Bowen, Ian Gregson. My daughters Rebecca and Kelsey have, as always, been amazingly generous and supportive, always ready to help with the switches and dials on my steam-operated PC. As ever, special thanks and love to my partner and sometime co-translator, Yurij Drobyshev: he made poems and peace and happiness possible for me for more than 30 years. He died while I was putting this collection finally together: it is for him.